Number Fun

Written by Charlotte Raby
and Emily Guille-Marrett
Illustrated by Laura González

Collins

1

2

2

1–5

6

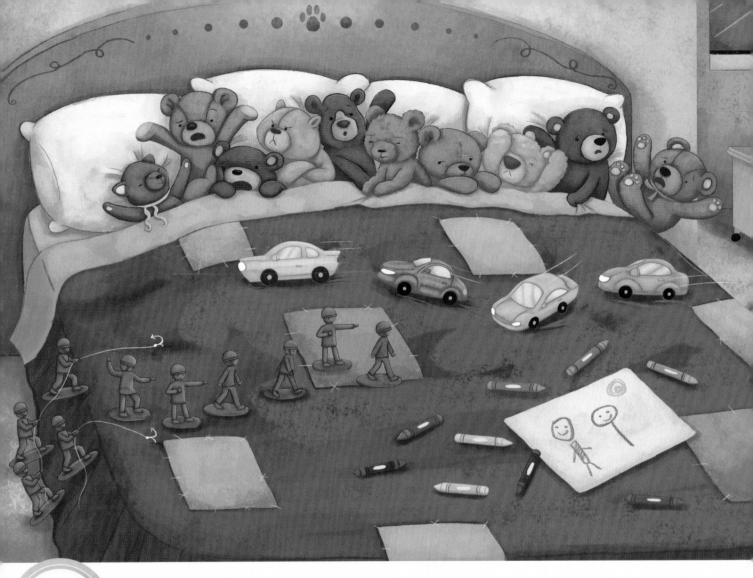

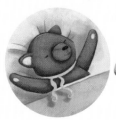

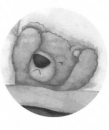

11

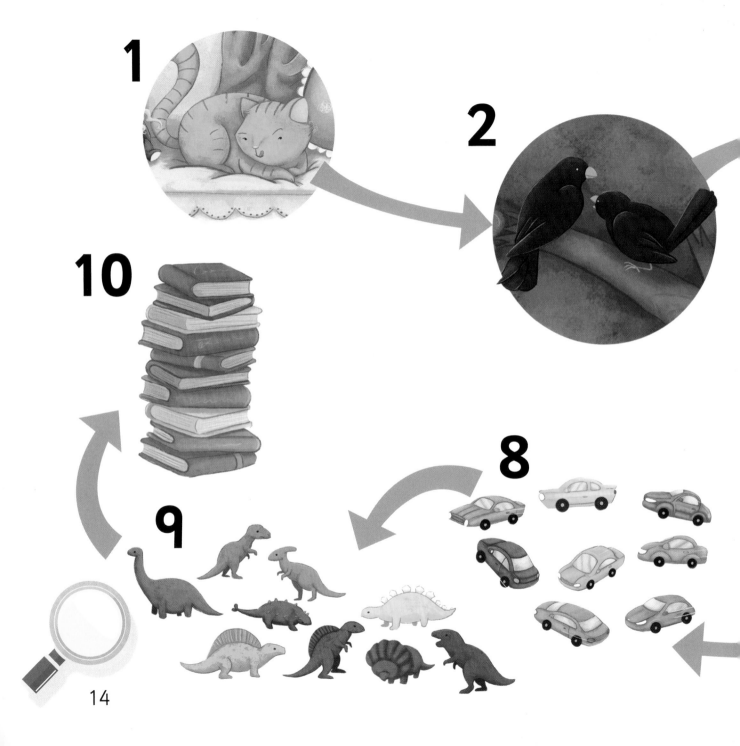

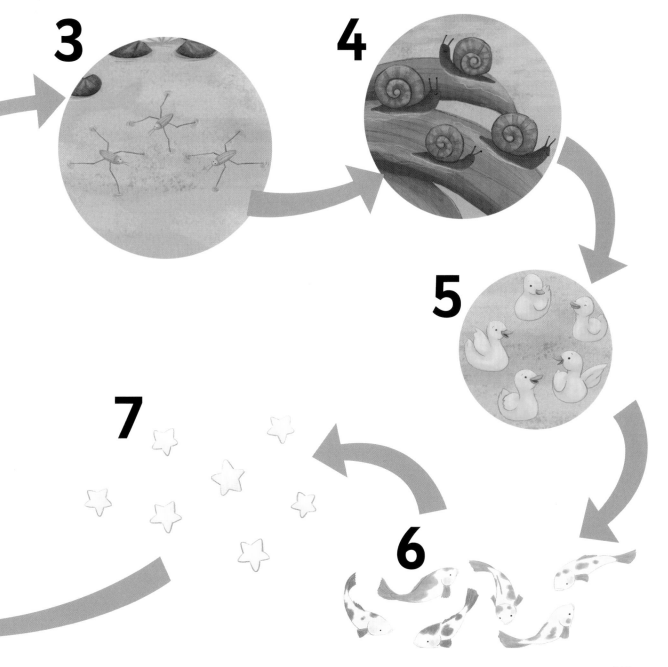

3

4

5

7

6

 Review: After reading

Read 1: Decoding
- Say the sounds in the words below. Ask the children to repeat the sounds and then say the word.

  b/e/d   bed   c/u/p   cup   d/u/ck   duck

  c/a/t   cat   t/e/d   ted
- If the children cannot work out what the word is, say the sounds, and then say the word. Ask the children to repeat after you.
- Challenge the children to find amounts of each object in the story, e.g. *two teds*.

Read 2: Prosody
- Encourage the children to hold the book the right way up and turn the pages.
- Let them explore the pages and tell you their version of the story, using the pictures for support.

Read 3: Comprehension
- Look at pages 10 and 11. Can the children work out what the little ted is doing?
- Say/sing *There were ten in the bed* …
- For every question ask the children how they know the answer. Ask:
    o Is the little ted being kind?
    o Do you think the other teddies mind?
    o Do you ever play games like this?